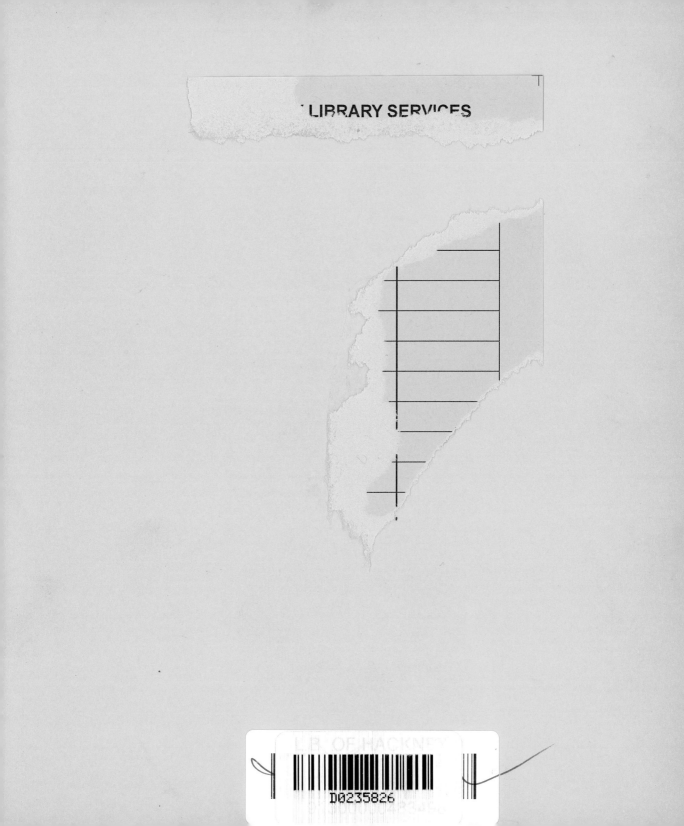

Living and Non-living in the

Mountains

Rebecca Rissman

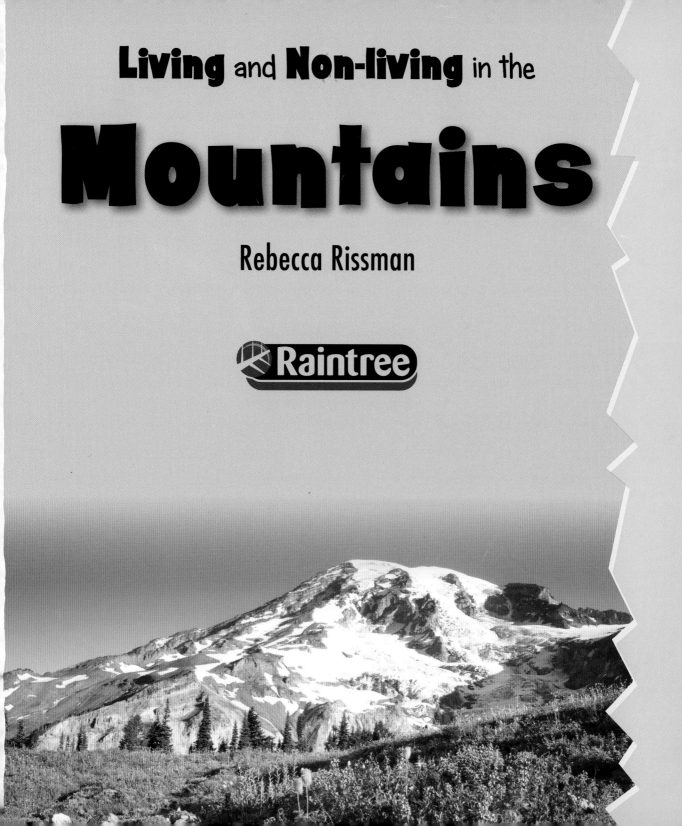

Raintree is an imprint of Capstone Global Library Limited, a company incorporated in England and Wales having its registered office at 7 Pilgrim Street, London, EC4V 6LB – Registered company number: 6695582

To contact Raintree:
Phone: 0845 6044371
Fax: + 44 (0) 1865 312263
Email: myorders@raintreepublishers.co.uk
Outside the UK please telephone +44 1865 312262.

Text © Capstone Global Library Limited 2014
First published in hardback in 2014
The moral rights of the proprietor have been asserted.

Edited by Daniel Nunn, Rebecca Rissman, and Catherine Veitch
Designed by Cynthia Della-Rovere
Picture research by Tracy Cummins
Production by Sophia Argyris
Originated by Capstone Global Library Ltd
Printed and bound in China by Leo Paper Products Ltd

ISBN 978 1 406 26593 4
17 16 15 14 13
10 9 8 7 6 5 4 3 2 1

British Library Cataloguing in Publication Data
A full catalogue record for this book is available from the British Library.

Acknowledgements
We would like to thank the following for permission to reproduce photographs: Getty Images pp. 14 (© Joseph Van Os), 18 (© Klaus Nigge); Shutterstock pp. 1, 21 (© Christopher Boswell), 4, 23a (© Rigucci), 5 (© Standa Riha), 6 (© Eduard Kyslynskyy), 7 (© Ekaterina Pokrovsky), 8, 23d (© Galyna Andrushko), 9, 23c (© Jiri Vavricka), 10 (© Popova Valeriya), 11, 23b (© µ), 12 (© Paul Aniszewski), 13 (© Sergey Toronto), 15 (© Dennis Donohue), 16 (© SergeyIT), 17 (© Joel Whitaker), 19 (© Wendy Nero), 20 (© Asaf Eliason), 21 (©Christopher Boswell), 22 (© pixy).

Front cover photograph of a mountain goat with kid in Utah, USA reproduced with permission of Superstock (© Animals Animals).

We would like to thank Michael Bright and Diana Bentley for their invaluable help in the preparation of this book.

Every effort has been made to contact copyright holders of material reproduced in this book. Any omissions will be rectified in subsequent printings if notice is given to the publisher.

All the Internet addresses (URLs) given in this book were valid at the time of going to press. However, due to the dynamic nature of the Internet, some addresses may have changed, or sites may have changed or ceased to exist since publication. While the author and publisher regret any inconvenience this may cause readers, no responsibility for any such changes can be accepted by either the author or the publisher.

Some words are in bold, **like this**.
You can find them in the glossary on page 23.

Contents

What is a mountain?

A mountain is a rocky, tall **landform**.

Mountains are very large.

Different types of plants and animals live in the mountains.

There are **non-living** things in the mountains, too.

What are living things?

Living things are alive. Living things need air and **sunlight**. Living things need food and water.

Living things grow and change.

Living things move on their own.

What are non-living things?

Non-living things are not alive. Non-living things do not need air and **sunlight**.

Non-living things do not need food or water.

Non-living things do not grow and change on their own.

Non-living things do not move on their own.

Is a pine tree living or non-living?

A pine tree needs water.

A pine tree moves on its own towards the sun.

A pine tree grows and changes.

A pine tree needs air and **sunlight**.

A pine tree is **living**.

Is ice living or non-living?

Ice does not move on its own.

Ice does not grow.

Ice does not need food.

Ice does not need air or **sunlight**.

Ice is **non-living**.

Is a mountain lion living or non-living?

A mountain lion grows and changes.

A mountain lion needs food and water.

A mountain lion moves on its own.

A mountain lion needs air and **sunlight**.

A mountain lion is **living**.

Is soil living or non-living?

Soil does not move on its own.

Soil does not need food or water.

Soil does not grow on its own.

Soil does not need air or **sunlight**.

Soil is **non-living**.

Is an eagle living or non-living?

An eagle grows and changes.

An eagle needs food and water.

An eagle moves on its own.

An eagle needs air and **sunlight**.

An eagle is **living**.

Is a wild flower living or non-living?

A wild flower moves on its own towards the sun.

A wild flower needs water.

A wild flower grows and changes.

A wild flower needs air and **sunlight**.

A wild flower is **living**.

What do you think?

Is this rock **living** or **non-living**?

Glossary

landform natural shape in the land

living alive. Living things need food and water. They breathe and move on their own. They grow and change.

non-living not alive. Non-living things do not need food or water. They do not move on their own. They do not grow and change on their own.

sunlight light from the sun

Find out more

Websites

Click through these images of living and non-living things, then take a quiz!
www.bbc.co.uk/schools/scienceclips/ages/5_6/ourselves.shtml

Look for eight living things in this pond scene!
www.bbc.co.uk/schools/scienceclips/ages/8_9/habitats.shtml

Check out this site to learn more about what living things need.
www.kidsbiology.com/biology_basics/needs_living_things/living_things_have_needs1.php

Books

About Habitats: Mountains, Cathryn Sill (Peachtree Publishers, 2009)

Living and Nonliving, Carol K. Lindeen (Capstone Press, 2008)

Index